Published by R-Cool Communications, Madison, WI

R-Cool Communications books can be purchased in bulk at a reduced rate. Please call 888-993-2355 for more information.

Printed in the United States of America.

BEYOND PAPER OR PLASTIC
8 Items or Less to Remarkable Service

With Professional Speaker
Rob Bell

Dedication

My love for Remarkable Service was developed while working with Dick Brodbeck, the founder of Dick's Supermarkets, Inc. His passion for treating everyone with respect and appreciation was inspiring and infectious.

Dick passed away in 1983 and his sons Bob and Barry picked up right where Dick left off. Without the support and encouragement from Bob and Barry, I would not be on the road sharing the people skills that all who worked with Dick's Supermarkets lived and breathed every day.

My wife Carrie and son Craig continue to provide the support and encouragement that keeps me on the road. Their belief in what I do gives me the energy and enthusiasm that allows me to get up front, have a party and let 'em watch.

"Absolutely Everything Counts"

About The Author

Rob Bell began teaching his customer service and communication techniques early in his tenure as Personnel Development and Education & Training Director for Dick's Supermarkets, Inc. Drawing on 25+ years of experience in leadership roles, customer service, and training, Rob makes it simple, clear and FUN to improve customer service and gain leadership skills.

Before becoming Dick's Supermarkets' go-to-guy for training, as a recovering CPA, Rob worked as the accounting manager for a large transportation company, an auditor, and an adjunct instructor at the University of Wisconsin - Platteville. Rob now tours the country teaching the principles that have helped hundreds of companies and organizations improve their communication strategies.

Rob's warmth and humor shine through in each presentation, allowing participants to gain insight into numerous aspects of corporate communication while giving them the tools to bring that insight into action.

Now Rob brings his high power message to companies world-wide. Rob's presentations are high-energy and feature real-life anecdotes that are as fun as they are meaningful. Participants leave Rob's presentations "fired up" and supplied with the techniques they need to meet and exceed company goals and expectations.

Rob's wide array of presentations are fully customized and are available in keynote, seminar, or workshop format.

Visit **www.RobSpeaks.com** for more information.

"If we don't take care of the Customer,
someone else will."

Chapter One
Moments of Truth

Have you ever experienced lousy Customer Service?

I know, I know. You're thinking, "Duh! Of course I have. I sure hope this book gets better fast."

You need to know the positive side of lousy Customer Service. When it is committed (Yes…I said committed) by your competitor, it enables you to win the comparison war. Trust me on that one. All of us, consciously or not, are continually practicing what is known as the connoisseur effect. That is—we compare everything to the best that we've ever experienced.

All you have to do is provide reasonable Customer Service to stand out from the crowd. Imagine what occurs when you are the creator of Remarkable, Fantastic Customer Service! You will be hailed as a Rock Star in a world of amateurs.

Every contact with another person is a Moment of Truth.

These Moments of Truth provide opportunities to polish or tarnish your personal and professional reputation. I'm sure you've heard that the most effective form of advertising is word-of-mouth. Of course, that advertising can be either negative or positive. Job One for you is to ensure with everything in your power that your word-of-mouth advertising is positive.

Moments of Truth fall into three categories:

- A Moment of Misery. Dropping the ball and not meeting customer expectations.
- Average Moment. Leads to Satisfied Customers. How BORING!

- Moments of Magic. Moments of Magic are where your Long-Term Success lives.

Moment I: Moment of Misery

A couple of years ago I stayed at a hotel in Denver, CO. I got into my room about 8:00 p.m. without having eaten dinner. I ordered a hamburger from room service and decided to get comfortable by jumping into a pair of sweatpants. Pulling out two dollars to give as a tip, I realized that the sweatpants didn't have any pockets. So I placed the money on the desk and waited. And waited. And waited.

Finally—a knock on the door.

I grabbed the two bucks and opened the door only to find a young man standing there with an extremely blank look on his face. His shirt, which was only partially tucked in, had ketchup stains smeared all over it.

Despite the fact that I was both tired and hungry, I smiled and said "Hi, how're you doing?"

He stared at me for a very long moment before letting out a sigh and jolted me with his reply, "This job totally sucks, man. I hate it!"

Now I've got a dilemma. I've got these two dollars out that he probably doesn't deserve and nowhere to hide them.

So I figure, what the heck? He probably can use the two bucks so I handed him the tip. He almost smiled. Not quite—but almost.

"Do you believe it, man? This is the first tip I've gotten all day!?"

"No, really?" I thought. "I can't imagine why."

Some people should not be in the Service Industry. I can tell if you love your job or not. If you ask a person who is not a Service Professional how his day is going, the response you'll get will probably include him looking at his watch and then responding "It'll be a lot better in about forty-seven minutes."

Yep, that's a pro. You can tell that he would rather be anywhere else on the planet than providing service. It's not that he's a bad person. He's just in the wrong line of work.

First Impressions

As the old saying goes, "We only have one chance to make a first impression." First impressions are important to take seriously.

If my first impression of you or your business is negative, I don't think you care, I don't think you're competent, and/or I don't think you're on the cutting edge — I will battle hard to defend that negative first impression.

After my less-than-stellar experience with Delivery Dude, I started looking for more negatives to reinforce my first impression. I got on the elevator and noticed that the ceiling tiles were dirty. I noticed that when I met other hotel employees in the halls, none of them made eye contact, smiled, or greeted me.

It was then that I realized Delivery Dude was right…this place really does suck. There's always somewhere else to do business. I sure won't be staying at that hotel again.

On the other hand, if my first impression is "WOW, this place is great! My service provider is sincerely friendly," I will see the positives and ignore many difficult situations. I mean, they don't say love is blind for nothing.

As long as I can remember I have always had a passion for Remarkable Customer Service. When I receive fantastic service I make it a point to congratulate the service provider personally. And then I make sure to tell as many people as possible that if they need that service or product, they must check out this place.

My dad's a great guy. I love him a lot. I am very proud of the success he's had as a cattle buyer.

But Dad is a cowboy. He'd rather shoot you than serve you. I mean, I'm lucky to have gotten out alive. Dad would rather sort cattle than serve people. I, on the other hand, LOVE to serve people and it shows. That's what is great about our economy…we have choices. If you don't love serving people, do something else.

Moment II: Average Moment

Average Moments just don't count. We all have so much going on, so much noise, that we don't remember average.

If you had dinner a week ago and it was just an average experience, I'll bet you a buck (it would be more, but my wife, Carrie, is my CFO and VP of Everything, so I don't have access to more cash) that you would not be able to tell me where you dined, let alone what you had for dinner.

Average does not stick in our memory banks. Average does not build loyalty. Average is boring.

Bottom line: Average happens by accident.

Moment III: Magic Moment

Magic Moments are the stuff that success is built on. Magic Moments build Loyalty.

A couple of years ago my wife, son and I decided to drive from Lancaster, WI to Denver CO. My son had just earned his driver's license and we thought that the drive would provide an excellent opportunity for Craig to hone his driving skills.

Quick aside: I don't know if you have ever driven on I-80 between Wisconsin and Colorado but it's a very busy highway. Craig took the wheel and before we were twenty-five miles down the road my wife screamed "I CAN'T TAKE IT ANY MORE!"

Personally, I thought he was doing pretty well. Carrie disagreed. So I got to practice my driving skills for about 1,775 miles.

Back to the experience: Before we embarked on our adventure I called the American Automobile Association.

A very friendly professional, named Mandy, answered the phone.

I said, "Hi Mandy, Rob Bell here. We are headed for Denver, CO from Lancaster, WI and would like to know how best to get there, road construction problems, and any other information you can provide."

Mandy asked "When are you leaving, Mr. Bell?"

"One week from today" I replied.

Mandy, exhibiting her Professional Service Skills, said, "I'll put a rush on the information so that you have time to plan."

"Mandy, you're great," I said.

Mandy really got me pumped when she replied with sincere and friendly professionalism, "Mr. Bell, we're not great; we're AWESOME!"

I absolutely loved Mandy's Pride and Enthusiasm.

At the time, I was the Personnel Development/Education & Training Director (try fitting that on your business card) for Wisconsin-based Dick's Supermarkets, Inc. I immediately asked Mandy where she was located.

"I'm in Omaha, NE," she replied.

Shoot, we don't have any supermarkets in Omaha, or I would have tried to hire her away from AAA on the spot.

By the way, I did email Mandy's supervisor to let him know about her fantastic service and the Magic Moment she provided.

I truly believe that Mandy does her job very well because she is treated by her employer with respect and appreciation. You can't fake this stuff.

As I mentioned earlier, average happens by accident. Let me finish the thought by saying excellence happens on purpose.

"*Average Happens by Accident,*

Excellence Happens on Purpose."

It's those companies that really do sweat the small stuff that consistently deliver Magic Moments. They exceed Customer Expectations when opportunities present themselves and build the loyalty that earns long-term business success.

Bottom line: Every Moment of Truth is an opportunity to Polish or Tarnish our personal and professional reputations. It takes many acts to earn a great reputation and just a small act to destroy it. As the MasterCard ad might say, "Our Reputations are PRICELESS!"

Loyalty

Loyalty must be our goal when it comes to long-term business success. We are doing our Customers a huge service when we earn their loyalty. We all have many decisions to make every day. How should I spend my time effectively? Where should I go for the products and services that I need? How can I get the best value for my hard-earned dollars?

When we have earned the Loyalty of our Customers,

we've solved a myriad of their problems.

I always have my hair cut by Karen Reynolds at J-Pauls. My wife thinks I'm crazy to drive thirty-five miles round trip to get my hair cut, when I could just as easily and probably cheaper, get it done in my home town.

But Karen is a friend of mine. She has been cutting my hair for years. She knows how I like it cut (after all, you don't look this good by accident). She is interested in my professional success and I am interested in hers.

I tell Karen that I mention her in many of my seminars all over the United States. Unfortunately, she still charges me for my hair cuts. Oh well, she's worth it. She's my friend.

What I'm getting at is that all things being equal, people want to do business with friends. In fact, all things being not quite equal, people still want to do business with friends.

Loyalty happens when we care about the people,

businesses and organizations that we interact with.

The most Loyal Customers I have ever seen ride Harley Davidsons. That's Loyalty when you tattoo the Harley logo on your body. You are not going to see these guys riding around on a Suzuki...not that there is anything wrong with Suzukis.

"We only have one chance to make a first impression."

Chapter Two
Eight Items to Remarkable Service

Item One
Manage First Impressions.

As I mentioned earlier, first impressions are "sticky." If my first impression of you and your company is that you're organized, professional, friendly, helpful, knowledgeable, and clean. I will work hard to protect my first impression. It's human nature to want to "stick" with your first impression. In fact, I will give you a break when your service levels are not up to speed, at least the first time.

I just got my hair cut by Karen at J -Pauls today. Right

in the middle of my haircut, the phone rang and Karen picked it up. She proceeded to talk to the person on the other line for what seemed like five minutes.

If this was the first time that Karen was cutting my hair, I would have been less than impressed. In fact, I probably would have been offended and mad.

But since I have been visiting Karen every month for almost ten years, I knew that the call must be important, so I took it in stride.

The call was important. Her dog, Cocoa, had blown out his ACL (I think the dog must play football). Cocoa had surgery today and would have to stay overnight at the veterinary hospital. I won't say how much the surgery cost, since Karen's husband might read this book and I'm sworn to secrecy.

If my first impression with your company was less than a WOW, I will be quick to judge your service harshly. Our margin for error is very thin at first. The more Loyal your Customers are the more breathing room they will allow you.

Building Loyalty takes commitment, consistency, and time. Include your Team to develop proactive ways to earn that Loyalty. All of us are smarter than one of us.

Ask questions like:

- If you had a magic wand, what would you do to make doing business with our company even more enjoyable?
- What barriers are making it difficult to do business with us?
- What standards and policies are getting in the way of allowing us to provide Remarkable Service?

A quick warning: You are opening a can of worms when you ask these questions. I guarantee that it can be a valuable can of worms, but it's still a can of worms.

Don't ask the questions if you're not going to commit to making changes and communicating which will be made and why some will be put on hold.

Item Two
Keep it Clean.

Be very aware of your Customers' perceptions of cleanliness. When you work in the same location, you can quickly become "location blind." Because you are there day in and day out, it's easy to not see opportunities to add polish and sparkle to your place of business. In fact, it's easy to step over obstacles and accept a less-than-stellar environment.

How does your parking lot look? Are the lines painted on the pavement clear and fresh? Do you have a public waste basket or ash tray next to the front door that needs cleaning?

If your business uses yellow "Caution Wet Floor" signs, inspect them. Many times they become dirty because they're always in the middle of a mess.

How about your public restrooms? Are they really clean? Think about it, do you want to do business with a company that can't keep the restrooms clean? And I don't like those hourly checklists that are on the back of some restroom doors. I love to inspect the inspection process. I usually find that the whole day was checked off at once in advance or the checklist hasn't been used for days or even months. They look tacky.

I also think it's funny that many restrooms have signs posted that state something like "We care about keeping our restrooms clean. If our restroom needs attention for any reason, please report the situation to management." Really? Only management can deal with the situation? I would think that anyone working at the location would want to know and have the opportunity to resolve it.

Because restrooms are so susceptible to becoming dirty, I do suggest that someone be responsible to check them regularly. Just don't have a chart that everyone can see is not holding us responsible.

Introducing the Opportunity Walk

The magic of the Opportunity Walk happens when you ask a different person on your Team to conduct an inspection each week. You would be amazed at how many opportunities there are to add sparkle & polish to your Customers' experience.

When we include our whole team in changing the lens from which we view our business, we will all be watching for opportunities while we're working. Initially you will probably see quite a few issues that need addressing. However, when we conduct Opportunity Walks on a regular basis, the Sparkle and Polish opportunities will become harder to find.

Assignment I:

Go to my website *(robspeaks.com/opportunitywalk)* and print two copies or more of the Opportunity Walk form. Find at least one other person to conduct an Opportunity Walk at your business today. Do the Opportunity Walk at the same time, but don't walk together. Rather, conduct the inspection separately and then compare notes. I know that you will each see some Opportunities that the other person didn't notice.

Assignment II:

Now that you've just done a thorough inspection of the property, there is one more very important area to inspect...YOURSELF.

Inspect your personal appearance. Are you clean and neat? Shirt and pants are pressed or at least not wrinkled? I invested twenty five years in the supermarket business. There were times that I would encounter a Meat Guy that looked like he'd lost the patient. Meat Guys loved to tell me that it's juice, not blood.

WHO CARES? Change the jacket, please!

How's your breath? I recently visited my optometrist for an eye examination. Unfortunately for me, just before my appointment, I am certain that he had a smoke. If you've ever had an eye exam, you know how close the doctor gets to your face. I almost offered him a breath mint. Not wanting to be rude, I just held my breath. Remember...EVERYTHING COUNTS!

Item Three:
Keep it Friendly.

"Are you serious?" you're thinking. Of course we need to keep it friendly.

If keeping it friendly is so obvious, then you must have never been served by a rude person. I'm pretty sure you've had a less than stellar service provider some time in your life.

Friendly service requires that we make friendly a high priority. Friendly comes from the heart, not the head. I can tell if someone is faking it – they're being friendly because they were told to, not because they truly feel it.

Friendly makes positives very positive and negatives correctable. If you have an upset Customer approach you and you choose to maintain a level of professional friendliness, in most cases, that person will not be able to stay mad.

If you have been in the service industry for any length of time at all, I am sure that you have had the opportunity to serve Customers that were in a lousy mood. You can tell by their body language and tone of voice, this guy is upset.

You don't know why he's upset. Maybe he overslept and is running late, he burned his toast, his car wouldn't start, and then when it did he got a speeding ticket because he was running late.

You had nothing to do with his lousy day, but all of a sudden, through no fault of your own, you are stuck in the middle of his crisis.

By keeping in mind that you are responsible for your actions and reactions, you are able to maintain a sincerely professional and friendly demeanor. By not taking the situation personally, the Customer will quickly lose the negative energy. Before you know it, he will be apologizing for losing his temper. When you don't give the person a reason to push back, the negative energy quickly dissipates.

Just think of a QTIP...Quit Taking It Personally.

Item Four
Be accurate.

Relationships are built on TRUST. Being very careful to accurately fulfill our Customers' expectations goes a long way when it comes to earning that trust.

Be sure to never over promise and under deliver. Instead, focus on providing a UPOD: Under Promise – Over Deliver.

I know it's easy to say whatever it takes to get the Customer to leave you alone for the moment and promise the world. Sure we want to provide excellent service, but we also must be realistic. Be careful to promise only what we can deliver.

In other words, we must manage our Customers' Expectations. The following equations explain my point:

CE = Customer Expectation CP = Customer Perception

- If CE is greater than CP, the Customer will remember a bad experience and tell others
- If CE equals CP, the Customer was satisfied and won't tell others
- If CE is less than CP, the Customer will remember a great experience and tell others

Word-of-mouth advertising is the most effective form of advertising, either positive or negative. By managing expectations, we have the opportunity to also manage the word-of-mouth advertising that is out there. We definitely want to be Remarkable for providing excellent service.

A couple of years ago my wife and I bought a new car from a dealer in Madison, WI, which is about one hundred miles from our home. We live in a small town and enjoy visiting the "Big City" occasionally. However, I had concerns about being that far from the dealer's service center.

The salesman who sold me the car promised that every time I brought my car in for service, including oil changes, the dealership would be happy to provide a loaner car at no charge. Cool. We can have the car serviced and enjoy the beautiful city of Madison on a regular basis.

So, we spent a lot of money with the dealership and purchased the car.

When I called for the first oil change, I was unpleasantly surprised. I mentioned to the Service Department Lady that the salesperson promised that we could have a loaner car whenever I had my car serviced, including oil changes.

I was shocked when the woman who answered the telephone replied, "There is no way we're going to give you a loaner car for an oil change."

I couldn't believe my ears. I was very disappointed. I have told many friends to never purchase anything from this dealership and I can guarantee you that I will never do business there again.

Think about the opportunities that were lost by the salesperson who over-promised and under-delivered.

I love to drive and tend to buy a new car every four years. If we use an average retail of $25,000 for each one that I purchase and assume I will buy at least eight cars before they take my driving privileges away, the total lost sales to the dealership in Madison is $200,000. Bear in mind that doesn't include my friends who may have done business with them if I hadn't told them to stay away!

You can easily see the negative impact caused by one sales person who over-promised and under-delivered. The impact is HUGE.

Again, focus on being very accurate about the products and services that you offer and the cost the Customer will incur. Be sure that you only provide Unexpected Joy, not Unexpected Pain!

Item Five
Serve with a Sense of Urgency.

Have you ever walked into a store that has fifteen checkout lanes and only two are open with a crowd of frustrated Customers looking for anyone, please anyone in the world, to help them?

And then, to add insult to injury, you see a person that you know has the ability to open a checkout lane. Cool, you think, help is on the way. But instead, he tells his fellow cashiers that he's going on break. Yep, I know we've all been there.

When I was in college I worked at Dick's Supermarket in Platteville, WI. Dick Brodbeck, the incredible leader who started Dick's (funny coincidence that his name was Dick, too) had his office on the mezzanine of the store with a window that overlooked the front end.

Some of you probably remember the old registers. They had round number keys surrounded by the departments of Grocery, Dairy, Produce, etc. Back in those days, every item was individually price marked. The cashier always said the price out loud that she was keying so that the Customer knew he was being charged the right price. Remember, it was difficult to review your receipt back then because the item descriptions were not printed, just the department.

I still remember times when we would be very busy and Dick would come running down stairs and open a checkout lane, to the relief of the waiting Customers. Actually, many of our Customers would be impressed that Dick was actually checking them out.

The store manager, on the other hand, was not so thrilled. He would tell the front end manager with a sense of urgency, "Puuleez get Dick out of the checkout lane. NOW!"

The manager knew something the Customers didn't – Dick didn't know how to check!

Don't worry, he wasn't ripping people off. He just didn't know how to apply sales tax. The Customer was probably getting a better deal. Please don't turn him into the Wisconsin Sales Tax Police. Actually, we have probably exceeded the statute of limitations.

Working with Dick taught me the importance of serving with a Sense of Urgency. Dick always led by example. He demonstrated what I like to call Full Contact Customer Service. Dick would not allow barriers to get in the way of providing excellent service.

Over the years I have noticed that people are usually patient when they see and sense that you are serving them with focus, respect and that all-important sense of urgency.

As I'm writing today, we are having a pretty good snowstorm here in Wisconsin, expecting six to eight inches. I went shopping at the local supermarket this morning, and as expected due to the snowstorm, the store was packed. I am one of those people, who for some unknown reason gets hungrier when snow storms are predicted.

If you've ever had the responsibility of writing personnel schedules, you know how challenging the process is. At Dick's we always had the schedule posted at least ten days in advance so that people could plan their lives. That means that we were scheduling shifts as much as seventeen days in the future. Unfortunately, we never had access to weather forecasts that were accurate for that kind of a time-frame.

Snowscares are great for business, but can be challenging for the people who are working. On top of the unforeseen business that snowscares bring, they also make it difficult for some people to make it to work.

Because of these facts, I was impressed that every person who worked in the store was up front helping to get people served. I'm certain that they all had other tasks waiting to be done in their respective departments, but they were focused on getting us hungry-snowscared Customers served.

The sense of urgency they displayed made it much easier to stand in line and wait my turn to be served. And, they weren't complaining about how busy it was and how they had important things to get done. Again, I was impressed.

Actually, I love snowstorms. They are exciting.

It's funny how snowscares make people hungry...I know from experience that snowscares are great for business. Unfortunately, once the snow actually hits, the business dies. That's why grocers prefer snowscares over snowstorms. We used to consider calling the local radio station in the middle of the summer to see if they would announce a surprise summer snowstorm, just for the business and the fun of it.

When you make me wait to be served, whether in a checkout lane, on the telephone, or an email reply, you send a message that you don't respect my time or me.

Time is a non-renewable resource. Once you've wasted my time, I can't get it back. It's gone forever.

On the other hand, when you don't allow barriers to get

in the way, you show sincere appreciation that I have chosen you as my service provider.

As the old saying goes, "If we don't take care of the Customer, somebody else will."

Item Six
Be a great listener.

Have you ever been speaking to someone and had the feeling that they weren't listening?

Are you married?

Listening is an active skill. We hear with our ears. We LISTEN with our brains.

Studies indicate that we speak to ourselves at an amazing speed of between 400 and 600 words-per-minute.

Have you ever tried to go to sleep at night and not been able to get your brain to SHUT UP? You look at the alarm clock and think, "Oh my gosh I gotta be up in three hours and then I have that very difficult meeting I don't think I'm prepared for that very difficult meeting and I think that really rude Customer has an appointment first thing in the morning and then I have to get the budget numbers done and then I have that doctor's appointment - I hope it's nothing serious - and I have to be up in two hours and fifty minutes! What am I going to do?

On the other hand people speak at about 125 words-per-minute, with gusts up to 150.

I might be speaking to you at about 132 words-per-minute, while your brain is processing at 573 words-per-minute. Without even realizing it, your mind starts to wander. You start thinking that when you get done here you have to get gasoline for your car; you need to call home to see if there was anything interesting in the mail, and if that cat pooped on the rug again…. Then you realize that you have no idea what I was saying. How embarrassing!

I've been a terrible listener at times; I'll bet you have too.

Have you ever asked a person for her name, and between the time you ask for her name and the time she gives it to you, you forget to listen? "And your name is?" And then you think "I've got to get an oil change…Shoot, what did she just say? She just said her name ten seconds ago. Please, somebody use her name."

I was at a conference recently where everyone had name badges on lanyards (that's a fancy name for the ropes that hold the name badges) around their necks. The gentleman who was going to kick off my part of the program introduced himself to me. Instead of paying attention to his name, I was thinking about the details for my program. And then I realized I forgot to listen to the guy who is going to introduce me, and I don't even know his name.

So, as inconspicuously as possible, I looked down at his name badge. Great, wouldn't you know it; his badge was flipped over so I couldn't see his name.

Now what am I going to do? Thinking I would be clever, I asked my new friend, "How do you spell your name?"

"E. D."

I don't think I covered my lack of attention very well when I told Ed that I just wanted to know if he used one or two "d's" in his name.

So, don't try that technique. It's definitely better to consciously stay in the moment and really listen.

In fact, when you truly listen to others, you demonstrate respect for their ideas and experiences.

Dr. Stephen Covey identified Five Levels of Listening in his classic book, <u>The 7 Habits of Highly Effective People</u>. Below are Dr. Covey's five levels of listening, from worst to first:

5. **Ignoring** is the lowest level (and really isn't listening at all). I have walked into some businesses and observed employees who are more interested in each other's conversations than me. You've been there. "Where are we meeting after work?" I don't know, how about the bowling alley? Cool is Fred coming...?

I believe that we need to acknowledge people within ten seconds of entering our business. If you make me wait longer, I feel invisible.

I guess people who ignore Customers believe the old adage that says "If we don't take care of the Customer, maybe they'll quit bugging us."

4. **Pretend Listening** can get you in a lot of trouble. At times, my wife has been talking to me, and instead of really listening, I have been caught pretending to listen. Carrie is talking – I'm pretending to listen; Carrie is talking – I continue to pretend to listen. All of a sudden I hear her ask "What do you think?" Oh-Oh. I'm in trouble, so I reply "Yes," which rarely works. I've been busted.

Pretending to listen is disrespectful to your Customers, your family and your friends.

3. **Selective Listening** is next. Contrary to popular listening mythology, I don't believe that men use Selective Listening more than women do. I don't believe it's gender specific.

We all do it. We hear what we want to hear and disregard the rest.

Listening level numbers five through three do not build relationships. Ignoring, Pretending and Selective Listening may actually alienate and offend others.

Now, on to the good stuff.

2. **Attentive Listening** is important to building friendships and relationships. Attentive Listening requires a conscious effort to stay in the moment. In fact, you shouldn't even begin to form a come-back statement. Just stay still. Stay in the moment.

When you feel and hear your mind start to wonder, consciously choose to bring it back so that you can truly focus on what the individual is saying.

Have you ever noticed that the words "listen" and "silent" use the exact same letters? Remaining silent and staying in the moment allows you to focus on the other person.

When we are attentively listening to others, we show respect. We honor them.

Others will think you were a very interesting person because you showed interest in what they had to say.

1. **Empathic Listening** is the highest form of listening.

We not only want to understand the other person's words, we want to understand how they feel about what they are saying.

Empathic Listening is very important when dealing with an upset

Customer or Team Member. Empathic Listening takes the negativity right out of the equation.

My favorite habit is number five from Dr. Stephen Covey's book: The 7-Habits of Highly Effective People: "Seek first to understand, then to be understood."

It's human nature to want to be understood first. However, when we take the time and make the effort to seek first to understand the other person, we show respect.

I have never encountered a person who does not want to be treated with respect.

Item Seven
Run to the Opportunity.

Many companies brag that their goal is to exceed their Customers' expectations. Exceeding Customer expectations is a lofty goal, but very difficult to achieve with every service interaction.

When a Customer has a problem, realize that this is

an opportunity to exceed his expectations. Run to the opportunity. By being a problem solver, you have the opportunity to enhance your personal and professional reputation. Plus it feels great when you know you went the extra mile.

I remember an opportunity to earn a WOW that happened at noon on a Friday in 1992. I was working in Dick's Supermarket of Lancaster, WI. The Team Member who was loading our Customers' cars, Cager (that was his nickname – don't ever call him Roger), called me to the front of the store and said "There is a lady in the parking lot and she is like freaking out."

"Oh great, now what?" I think. I venture outside, with trepidation and concern, wondering what the heck is going on.

Standing next to her car was a very upset young lady, crying and repeating "What am I going to do? What am I going to do?"

I look down and right next to her car I see what moments

before had been a beautiful birthday cake, but is now a heap of ant food.

She was hysterical and told me that her son was having his 6th birthday party later that afternoon. "I carried the cake to my car, instead of asking for help because I didn't want someone to drop the cake, and now I've ruined the party," she cried.

"Opportunity" I think.

I asked if she would have time to come into the store for a couple of minutes. She screamed, "I DON'T HAVE TIME TO COME INTO THE STORE!!!"

Whoa. She really is UPSET!

I explained that if she would allow me five minutes, I would do my very best to get another birthday cake for her son.

This calmed her down a little bit, not totally, but a little bit, and she said "Really?"

"Yes, come into the store and I will call the central bakery to see what our options are."

On the way in I asked for her name, and she replied that it was Teresa (the name has been changed to protect...you know the rest).

I called the central bakery and they said that they could have a replacement cake ready in one hour. I instructed them to proceed.

I then asked Teresa for the starting time of the party.

"Six o'clock,"

I promised her that we would deliver a cake to her house by four o'clock.

I lied.

When I knocked at the door at three o'clock, fresh birthday cake in hand, she was ecstatic to have the cake an hour earlier than expected. When she offered to pay for the replacement, I told her that she had already paid for a birthday cake and we would not accept a second payment.

And now for the payoff: I was working in the Lancaster store in the year 2000, when she saw me. I hadn't seen Teresa since her son's birthday in 1992.

She ran up to me and with excitement said, "It's great to see you, Rob. I still remember the day you saved my life."

Now, that's a greeting that caught my attention. I had no idea what she was talking about.

"Saved your life?" I replied.

"You must remember that day when I dropped Joey's six year birthday cake in the parking lot. Joey is now fourteen years old, so that's eight years ago. It felt like you saved my life by getting a replacement cake to my house in time for the party."

"Oh yeah, I did save your life that day," I joked. "I'm glad everything worked out. It's great to see you."

Isn't that amazing? That problem became an opportunity to earn an eight-year halo. I have to admit, I was gratified that Teresa remembered the event.

When you start each day, be on the lookout for opportunities to go the extra mile, or even the extra foot.

I believe that when you do something extra for another person you feel as good as or even better than the person you just helped. It's a positive perpetual motion event. When you give more than you get, you get more than you give.

Some people call opportunities problems, but thinking of problems as opportunities is a powerful paradigm shift.

Item Eight
Be Knowledgeable

Have Great Product Knowledge.

If a Customer asks a question that you don't know the answer, what should you do? Of course, the answer is to admit that you don't know, but you will find the answer. Don't use the MSU method – Make Something Up.

The more you know about your company, the more value you can provide. We want to provide helpful service not a "Hard-Sell." Everything that we offer to our Customers must be focused on their benefit first.

Ask yourself, are you offering the products that your Customers want to buy as opposed to the products that you want to sell? In other words, determine what your Customers want and give it to them!

Know Your Services.

We live in very fast moving times. Change keeps

happening faster and faster. Because of these changes, you probably offer services and products that your Customers are not aware of. By listening carefully to your Customers to really understand their individual needs, you have the opportunity to offer suggestions that will make their lives easier and more efficient.

When you make a person's life better, you earn their loyalty.

Know Your Community.

It's also important to know your community. When someone asks where the closest Automatic Teller Machine is, you should know the answer. When a person says she has never been in your community before, what's there to do; you sure don't want to say "There isn't much to do around here. If I was you I'd get back in your car and head to the next town."

By giving that kind of response, you undercut your whole community. The more professional response is to tell the person of upcoming events, great restaurants, and local attractions that people enjoy. In other words, be prepared so that you can provide useful and positive information.

"When you give more than you get,

you get more than you give."

- Rob Bell

Chapter Three
Building Relationships
We are in the people business.

Empathy

Empathy is the ability to put ourselves in another person's shoes. We are all a little different – thank goodness. The world would be a boring place if we weren't different. It's important to celebrate differences.

I'm sure you've heard of the Golden Rule: "Do unto others as you would have them do unto you."

The Golden Rule is a great rule that has been around a long time.

When it comes to providing Excellent Service, however, we need to crank it up a notch to the Platinum Rule: "Treat people the way they want to be treated."

As I write this, I'm a fifty-two year old man from Wisconsin who wears a piece of cheese on his head on Sundays. Those cheese-heads are a good look, but they do ruin your hair. Odds are good that you don't wear a piece of cheese on Sundays. That doesn't mean that you're weird, it just accentuates that we're different (and you're cheering for the wrong football team – Go Packers!).

It's amazing how we make snap judgments based on how others look. You've heard statements like the following:
"You know how young people are; they just don't know how to show respect."
"You know how old people are; they think they know it all."
"You know how rich people are..."
"You know how poor people are..."
"You know how (White, Black, Hispanic, Asian) people are..."

Bottom line, we're all in this together. Nobody is better

than anyone else.

I have never met anyone who does not want to be treated with respect. I have never heard anyone say "That lady is so respectful. She drives me nuts."

When it comes to building relationships, it starts with being sincerely respectful of others.

Instead of treating others the way you want to be treated, focus on treating others the way they want to be treated.

Body Language

Your body language is a walking billboard of your brand. Are you fully equipped with all of the options or a low-priced generic model? Your body language gives people their first indication of your brand.

Studies have shown that people who walk faster than average are perceived to be more intelligent. So even if you don't know where you're going...hit it. I've said to myself, "I have no idea where I'm going, but I am making good time getting there."

Now I don't want you to be pushing people out of the way just to look smart, but I'm sure you've encountered people who look less than professional.

On a hot afternoon in July, my son and I stopped at a little store known for having the best ice cream in the county. The guy wielding the ice cream scoop caused me to pause and question whether we really needed an afternoon snack.

He had tattoos all over both arms. I know that tattoos are popular these days, and I don't mean to be a prude, but this guy had some statements permanently displayed that I hope my son didn't read. His apron was filthy, his eyes were bloodshot, he was half-shaved, and, well, he just plain looked pretty scary.

As we walked in he yawned and complained "I've been working here since 10:30 this morning. I can't wait to be done."

Wow! Since 10:30 this morning, I think. I looked at my watch and realized it was 1:30pm. I can see why this guy was tired because he had already worked three whole hours. Now that's a tough shift. How does he do it?

Yep, this guy was a real Professional. I would estimate the gentleman to be in his late 40's and I'm not surprised that he has not moved up the ladder of success just based on his walking billboard.

Have you ever noticed that the vast majority of advertisements for analog watches (watches with hands) are pictured with the time set at ten minutes after ten? Right now, go find a magazine that has advertisements for watches. I'll bet you that most of the watches are pictured at ten minutes after ten.

The reason that the watches are pictured at ten minutes after ten is the hands are in the shape of a smile. It's a subliminal message so that you will like their products more.

Human beings like the shape of a smile. It makes us feel better when we smile and it makes others feel better when we smile at them.

In 1999, I went to China to see my best friend from college. Flying to China is one long flight. It was eighteen hours from Minneapolis to Shanghai. At about the nine-hour mark I didn't think I could take being cooped up on the plane anymore.

When we finally landed, I couldn't wait to get off of the airplane. I still remember how amazed I was to see Chinese people all over the place. I mean, there were like a billion of them. It was then that I realized that smiles are international. The people in China couldn't have been friendlier. When they exhibited a smile on their walking billboard, it always indicated that they were friendly, nice, and happy to see me.

Ideas to include on your Walking Billboard:
♦ Sincere Smile.
♦ Walk with a bounce in your step.
♦ Take the lead. Greet others and extend your hand

first.

♦ Shake hands firmly. Much can be conveyed by your handshake.

♦ Eye contact that tells others that you're interested in them.

♦ Get an eye, give 'em a "Hi."

♦ Lean forward. An almost imperceptible forward tilt will very subtly indicate your interest-in and openness-to the other person

♦ Maintain positive thoughts – people can read our mind

Studies indicate that we judge others based on their body language within seven seconds. That first seven seconds can make or break your reputation.

When it comes to Remarkable Customer Service we need to be very aware of the body language we present to our Customers. Excellent service and multi-tasking do not go together. People can tell by your body language if they are your first priority.

I walked into a department store to buy a tent that was

on sale for my son a few years ago. When I entered the store, I saw a sales clerk who was building a display of small gas grills in the front of the store.

I approached him and asked where the tents pictured in the advertisement were located. I can't tell you his name because he didn't bother to turn and make eye contact or greet me. No. He was too busy for that. Instead he kept building the display and said with an exasperated tone of voice "They're back by Sporting Goods."

I would have guessed that the tents would be back by Sporting Goods, I thought. The problem was that I didn't know where the Sporting Goods were.

His body language and tone of voice definitely put me in my place. He was too busy to help me, a potential Customer, who just wanted to spend money in his store to help pay his wages.

I was so offended by his demeanor that I decided that I would buy the tent at the department store down the street at full retail. This clerk turned an opportunity into a problem called Lost Sales.

A professional sales clerk would have stopped what he was doing, faced me, smiled, listened carefully, and then actually would have taken me to the tents. Sure, it would have taken a little bit more time. But the time spent would have been an investment in our relationship and in building his reputation.

Actions speak louder than words.

Remember, this life is not a dress-rehearsal. The curtain is up. This is show biz baby and we're on stage. Take responsibility for your body language – your "Walking Billboard."

Positive Words

I always ask the people in my audiences, "Who would you rather be around, a positive person or a negative person?"

Their response is consistently, "Positive!"

Once in a while there is a poor soul who wants nothing to do with positive people. I just choose to stay away from that person.

Misery loves company, but us positive people are having a party.

The words we choose are extremely important to the message we send. "Really Rob, are you sure?" you think. Yep. I'm positive.

Have you ever asked somebody, "How's it going?" And they respond with negative body language and tone of voice, "It's going."

Or when you ask a Teammate, "How was your vacation?" and she says, as if she's bummed out to be back, "Too short."

These all-too-common responses are not what I would consider positive.

When you ask a person how he's doing and he responds, "I'm so mad at my boss I don't know what I'm going to do, my son got another speeding ticket, and I have these nasal polyps that I think are contagious. What do you think?"

Whoa, you think. That's way more information than I needed. I really didn't care. I was just trying to be nice.

Ninety percent of the people who ask how you're doing are just being nice. They really don't want to know. The remaining ten percent probably think you deserve all of the problems you're whining about.

I suggest that you respond to "How's it going?" with a friendly "Great, thank you." "How was your vacation?" could be responded to with "Super, but it's great to be back to work with the Team." You get the idea - most people want to be around positive people. So choose to be a positive person.

Yes beats no. "Let me see what I can do" is much better

than "It's against our policy." The word policy is a trigger that raises Customers' defenses. They immediately get ready for battle. I prefer the word standard over policy.

When using the word standard, we need to explain why the standard is in place. The standard had better be in place for the Customer's benefit. For example, "Please be sure to buy only the amount of hamburger buns you need for your event. To ensure that the food you purchase from our store is safe, we have a standard where we do not accept returns of buns because the package seals cannot be verified. Of course, you can always freeze excess buns for future use."

If the standard can't be explained, I suggest that the standard needs to be reviewed. Maybe it's no longer applicable and we're putting up a barrier to Remarkable Customer Service.

When it comes to standards, the world is not black and white. We need to do what's right for the Customer. To provide Remarkable Service, we must use a good dose of Common Sense with the standard.

What's a good response to "Thank you?"

I bet you said "You're welcome." I agree. Additional positive responses to "Thank you" include "My pleasure." and "Thank you." These are all good.

Many times I hear less than stellar responses to thank you, such as "Yup" and "No problem."

"No problem" has two negative words built in...can you spot them? Look closely and you will see "No" and "Problem." Since everything counts, I strongly recommend that you choose not to use these words in a professional environment.

If a Customer says, "Gee, I hope I didn't cause you a problem," don't respond with, "You're welcome." In this situation, I recommend you respond with something like, "No problem at all. Glad I could help. Let me know how I can help in the future."

The following is a chart that compares responses:

The Power of Positive Words

Positive Words	Negative Words
Yes. Of Course. Certainly, Fine, OK.	No. Maybe not. Unh-unh. I don't know.
May I help you?	What do you want?
You can… I can… We could…for you.	You can't… I can't… You'll have to…/I'll have to…
Let me check. Let me ask.	They won't let me do that. It's against our POLICY.
Please. Thank you.	

In a professional environment it's important to choose your language carefully.

I started working at Dick's Supermarket in Dodgeville, Wisconsin on Wednesday December 27, 1972 at the age of seventeen. I was a very shy young man when I joined the Team and working with people really helped me come out of my shell.

Before long, I had really embraced serving Customers. Serving Customers provided a sense of confidence. I was definitely in my element and had found what I was naturally good at.

After working at Dick's of Dodgeville for two years I transferred to Dick's of Platteville because I was going to school at the University of Wisconsin – Platteville.

I was thrilled to be working at Dick's of Platteville. It was the biggest and fanciest store in the company. In fact Dick Brodbeck, the fantastic leader who founded the company, had his office on the mezzanine of the store.

"Man this is so great. Maybe I'll get to know Dick," I remember thinking. I had met Dick a couple of times when he toured the Dodgeville store, but I sure didn't know him. "This is going to be great!"

I had been working at Dick's of Platteville about two weeks when the bookkeeper, Joan, called me up front to the bookkeeper's office and asked, "Would you be able to take a delivery today?"

Cool, I thought! I get to drive around town in the company station wagon…we didn't have minivans back then.

"I'd love to take a delivery," I responded.

"Great, I need you to take a delivery to Hardees."

"Hardees? Are you kidding? You can see Hardees from the parking lot. I thought I was going to get to drive around town," I whined.

Joan thought for a moment and said, "Well, do you want to make the bank deposit, too?"

"Whoa. Are you kidding me? I'd be happy to make the bank deposit." I was totally PUMPED. Man, they must think I'm good. They trust me to make the bank deposit for the biggest store in the company.

With a bounce in my step I loaded the car while thinking, "I am having a great day. I love this job."

I drove down the street to Hardees, unloaded the delivery, got back in the car, started the car, and then to my dismay, I realized THE BANK DEPOSIT BAGS ARE GONE!!!

How could this be? I looked under the seat, between the seats, in the glove compartment. Oh my gosh, THE BANK DEPOSIT BAGS ARE GONE!!! I know Joan gave me two bags and THEY'RE GONE!!!

I got out of the car, looked under the car – nothing. I looked on top of the car and lying on the roof was ONE of the two bank deposit bags. "Nice job, moron," I thought to myself. I left the bank deposit bags on the roof of the car!!! And one of the bags is gone.

Oh my gosh, this can't be happening. How could anybody be so stupid?

I threw the one bag in the car, locked the car, and went running up the middle of the street, looking for the missing bag. I didn't find it.

All the time I kept thinking to myself over and over thoughts like "I'm an idiot. I'm a loser. This is the worst day of my life."

I went into the store and called for the store manager.

John came up front. Great! How do I tell the store manager that I had lost a bank deposit bag?

"Hi John," I say, "how's your day going?"

"It's going pretty well."

"Me too," I say. "John, I ah, I um, I lost one of the bank deposit bags."

"Excuse me?" John asked, agitated, excited, and potentially homicidal.

"I lost…"

John interrupted "You had better get out there and find it!"

"Yes sir."

And the next thing I knew John and I were outside looking under every car, bush, and rock for the missing bag when the next thing I know OUT WALKS DICK

BRODBECK. You know – the guy who founded Dick's Supermarkets...Our Father who art in Platteville.

"Oh no, somebody must have told Dick," I thought. "This is really a big deal. What an idiot, what a loser I am. This is the worst day of my life."

Dick says "Just keep looking. We'll find it."

I looked over and Dick was in the culvert and he was getting muddy.

"Loser. Idiot. Moron. Worst day of my life," I keep thinking to myself.

We didn't find the bank deposit bag and Dick finally said "Come on, let's get back to work. We're not going to find it. Rob, take the station wagon back to the store. John, you make what's left of the bank deposit."

Oh that hurt. Obviously I had lost Dick's trust.

When I got back to the store, I was not saying "Hi" to

Customers because I was having a Bad Day! I didn't know what was going to happen.

All of a sudden, I heard Dick Brodbeck say over the public address system, "Rob Bell come to the office please. Rob Bell to the office."

Oh no. It's over. I really liked working here. I just hope he makes it quick.

I walked into Dick's office and he said, "Have a seat."

I couldn't even look him in the eye as I say "I am so sorry. I am the biggest idiot in the world. I do not know how this could have happened."

Dick said with a calm, understanding voice, "You're not an idiot. You made a mistake. The only people in this world who don't make mistakes are those who don't do anything. On top of that, a gentleman found the bank deposit bag and he brought it back."

"Thank goodness," I said, relieved, but still wondering

what my future with Dick's Supermarkets was going to be.

"From now on you're in charge of making all bank deposits for Dick's of Platteville," Dick said.

"Are you kidding?"

"No, I'm not kidding," Dick replied with the kindest, most understanding smile I had ever seen. "If there is anybody who will keep his eyes on the bank deposit bags, it's you."

I remember that day like it was yesterday. Dick Brodbeck was a very powerful positive influence in my life. He was a fantastic coach, mentor and leader. I know that the best leaders are cheerleaders, and Dick sure knew how to get people fired up.

The "Bank Deposit Bag" is my signature story. I share that story in almost every presentation that I give. After numerous presentations, I have had individuals, usually managers, first, question whether this story is true, and second, tell me that they would have fired me. And I understand their comments.

I think these people are missing the point. As Dick said, "The only people in this world who don't make mistakes are those who don't DO anything."

Have you ever made a mistake? I'll bet you have. We all have. We're human beings. On the day I lost the bank deposit bag, I felt that I was the biggest idiot and loser in the world.

Question: Who is responsible for your thoughts? Answer: You are.

That terrible day that I lost the bank deposit bag, I was mentally beating myself up. I was saying terrible things to myself.

Dick's forgiving and encouraging support taught me to give myself a break.

Monitor your self-talk. What are you saying to yourself?

I mentioned earlier that we speak to ourselves at between 400 and 600 words per minute. We are what we think about most of the time. The most important conversations we have are with ourselves.

Only allow yourself a positive mental diet. Live with an attitude of gratitude.

Since 1999, my wife, Carrie, has been keeping a "Happiness Journal." Every day she writes down at least one good thing that happens to her. The entries don't have to be a big deal to make the Happiness Journal.

Examples have included entries such as:
- ► Went out to lunch with Ellen (our neighbor) and we had a great time
- ► Craig (our son) got a raise at work
- ► Found a penny (You do not want to get between my wife and a penny, she will take you out!)

The cool thing about Carrie's Happiness Journal is that the first entry on every page says "Thank goodness I married Rob Bell."

Well, it is in my handwriting. I mean you do need to be proactive!

How do you start your day? By saying statements to yourself such as:

> *"I'm so tired."*
> *"It's going to be a long day."*
> *"I don't want to go to work."*

If you start your day with negative statements the odds are that your day is going to be long, unfulfilled and you're going to be tired all day.

Instead start your day with positive statements such as:

"I'm alive."

"I'm awake."

"I feel great."

"I'm going to have a great day."

When you consciously choose to start your day in a positive way, you will have the energy to deal with the challenges that come your way. Oh yeah, you will also have a better day.

Dick Brodbeck taught to me to give myself a break. Only allow a Positive Mental Diet. I am confident that when you only allow a Positive Mental Diet, you will have more fun, enjoy life more, make more friends, be more successful; the list goes on and on.

Alright, so now that we're in a good mood, we're ready to discuss Complaints in the next Chapter.

"Complaining Customers are your most valuable Customers. They will tell you, free of charge, what you need to change."

Chapter 4
Turn Service Breakdowns Into Loyalty Building Opportunities

Have you ever had the opportunity to deal with an upset Customer? If you've been working in the "real-world" for long, you almost certainly have.

Complaint situations can be upsetting. Complaint situations are also great opportunities to exceed the Customer's expectations and earn Loyalty. In fact, studies have shown that people who complain to a business and have the situation professionally resolved are six times more likely to consider themselves Loyal, than people who have never complained.

Below is a "Complaint Quiz." Give it your best shot and then look at the answers and explanations on page 91.

Complaints Quiz

For each question, circle the one answer you think is correct.

1. What percent of unhappy Customers will complain to the business about rude or discourteous service?

   a. 48%   b. 4%   c. 11%   d. 24%

2. Of those Customers who don't complain to the business about rude or discourteous service, what percent will return to that business again?

   a. 10%   b. 30%   c. 20%   d. 50%

3. Of those Customers who do complain to the business, what percent are likely to return to that business again?

   a. 50%   b. 70%   c. 80%   d. 90%

4. About how much of their yearly sales volume do businesses lose due to poor service?

     a. 1%   b. 5%   c. 10%   d. 20%

5. How long can it take to change a poor service image?

     a. 2 yrs.   b. 1 yrs.   c. 5 yrs.   d. 10 yrs.

6. What is the biggest single reason businesses lose Customers?

     a. New competition.
     b. Indifferent employees
     c. Peer pressure.
     d. Dissatisfaction with the product

Complaint Answers

#1: The answer is letter b – 4%. Only about four percent of dissatisfied Customers will tell us about their disappointment. They won't tell the business, but they will tell their friends, neighbors, co-workers, and anyone else who will listen.

And every time they tell the story, the disappointment grows. It's not that they are lying. They're just making it more interesting – adding a little drama.

We can't afford to allow dissatisfied Customers to tell the world about how we dropped the ball.

You've probably heard "The Customer is always right." The reality is that the Customer is not always right. But, as a professional, our job is to make the person feel right. Many times it's easy to prove to the person that he's wrong. Maybe he didn't read the fine print, or the offer expired yesterday, or an infinite number of reasons we have let them down.

Which would you rather succeed at, winning the Customer's loyalty, or winning the argument? There is always somewhere else to do business.

#2: The answer is letter a – 10%. Only ten percent of dissatisfied Customers will give us another chance. That's a scary thought. Doing the math, we can turn the percentage around and realize that 90% of dissatisfied people don't need the stress and won't make the effort to tell us. They just won't come back.

#3: The answer is letter d – 90%. Ninety percent of the people who complain will give us another chance. Most people who complain are looking for reasons to continue doing business with us. Their thought process goes something like this:

"I've been doing business with Rob for years, and he's always treated me right. We all make mistakes. I'm going to let him know what happened."

When a Customer lets us know how we've dropped the service ball, we need to appreciate that he/she actually has gone the extra mile to find a way to continue doing business with us. Customer complaints are an opportunity to learn how we can improve our products and services.

#4: The answer is letter c – 10%.   On average, businesses lose about ten percent of their business due to poor service. That is a huge percentage that can be solved without additional expense to the business. All we need to do is care, sweat the small stuff, be nice, and be honest.

Customer service isn't rocket science. It's common sense. My guess is that I haven't shared any concepts that you didn't already know when it comes to providing fantastic service.   But the question is – are <u>YOU</u> consistently providing Remarkable Service?

The challenge for service professionals is providing consistently high "Make 'em Say WOW" service every day with every Customer.

#5: The answer is letter d – 10 Years. Yikes!! Ten years is a long time. Losing a bunch of Customers for ten years could easily mean the end of that business.

The problem is that people remember lousy service more than great service. Just one service break-down could easily end a Customer relationship. Once a person thinks we don't care or we're not honest or our services are not as good as the competition, we're in real trouble.

#6: The answer is letter b – Indifferent Employees.
Studies have shown that sixty-eight percent of people who report they have stopped doing business with a company do so as a result of indifferent employees.

They think "If you don't care, I don't care. You know more about this place than I do. I'm going to go where the people care and appreciate the opportunity to serve me."

I mentioned earlier that word-of-mouth is the most effective form of advertising. Word-of-mouth is even more important when it comes to the people working for our business. We all must be proud and enthusiastic about our business if we expect to be successful.

5.1 CLEAR Steps to Great Service.

1) Calm

2) Listen

3) Empathy

4) Apology

5) Remedy

5.1) Thank the person for letting you know

As the Complaint Quiz revealed, only four percent of dissatisfied Customers will tell US about their disappointment. Many times, the person who does let you know is upset and frustrated. He doesn't need this kind of stress, but darn it, he's going to let you know. He may even be prepared to GIVE YOU A PIECE OF HIS MIND!

Step 1: Calm. Consciously choose to remain Calm. When an upset person approaches it's natural to put up your defenses. You want to argue. Stop. Stay Calm. Breathing is good. It's a hobby of mine. Now is the time to make a personal choice not to get upset.

I'm not suggesting that you disconnect from the situation or the person. Instead connect and care.

Step 2: Listen. Listen without being judgmental. In Dr. Stephen Covey's book, "The 7 Habits of Highly Effective People," Dr. Covey says "Seek first to understand, then to be understood."

During the listening phase do not use "yeah-buts." You know what I mean, "Yeah-but two people called in sick;" "Yeah-but the warehouse was out;" "Yeah-but that's not my department." Upset Customers DO NOT WANT EXCUSES! They want to be heard.

Focus on fixing the problem, not the blame. Why we are out of the tuna that is on sale is not important. What's important is that we are out of the tuna and the Customer is disappointed.

When you truly listen without giving excuses, you are not pushing back and you are not providing the disappointed person any additional incentives to become upset. Remember, you can't control anyone but yourself.

Step 3: Empathy. When you put yourself in the other person's shoes, the negativity in the situation quickly disappears.

Saying something like, "Oh my gosh, I would be upset too," lets the person know you're on their side.

Be sure not to say, "I know just how you feel." Bottom line, you probably don't know how they feel and you're setting yourself up for the come-back line "You have no idea how I feel!"

When you use the first three steps, Stay Calm while sincerely Listening with Empathy, in most situations the negativity will dissipate.

There have been many times when I have had Customers who were initially upset say something like, "I'm sorry, I didn't mean to be a jerk."

Now YOU can respond, "No, you're not being a jerk. I apologize."

Oh yeah, that's the next step.

Step 4: Apology. The apology must be sincere. When your apology is sincere people can tell it's coming from your heart. You weren't told what to say. You're responding as a friend who wants to remedy the situation.

Step 5: Remedy. When we discussed choosing positive words, I mentioned that our success comes in Cans – not Cannots. Now is the time to tell the person what we can do. Then offer a couple of choices. You don't have to give the company away. But if you have effectively used the first four steps, the person has realized that he is being treated fairly by a true professional.

Most companies spend lots of money on advertising. The most effective form of advertising is word-of-mouth. Now is the time to invest in the relationship with this Customer. Now is a fantastic opportunity to exceed the Customer's expectations. You didn't make him jump through hoops. You didn't hide behind policies. Your words and actions made him feel respected. And people remember how they felt when doing business with you.

Step 5.1: Thank you. Congratulations. You've resolved the situation and made the Customer feel good about doing business with you. Be sure to say, "Thank you for bringing the situation to my attention. Please don't hesitate to contact me in the future if I can be of service."

I'll bet he will walk out thinking, "Wow! I have a friend who works here. I look forward to seeing (<u>Insert your name here</u>) the next time I visit."

Nice job. You just earned a halo. You made a new friend and built goodwill for you and your company.

Customer complaints can definitely be challenging. But when you approach the situation as an opportunity to build relationships and earn loyalty as opposed to thinking of the complaint as a problem, you set yourself and your company apart from the competition.

I'm never happy when we've dropped the service ball. However, I am aware of the loyalty-building opportunities that complaints bring to our business.

The next time you have the opportunity to work with a disappointed Customer, make it CLEAR that you are a professional.

Epilogue

Providing Fantastic Service takes more than just asking people if they want paper or plastic. It takes an attention to detail every day with every Customer. It requires that we look at every interaction with our Customers as an opportunity to make friends, build loyalty and earn the right to serve.

When you provide Remarkable Service, I guarantee you will not only help the other person feel good, you will feel great too. In fact, providing Fantastic Service is FUN.

It's a lot more fun to be excellent than mediocre.

If you provided mediocre or average service, you will probably drive home feeling tired, bored, and worn out thinking, "Bummer, I have to do this again tomorrow."

If you provided Remarkable Service, you may be a little tired, but you will also feel invigorated about the friends you made, and the Unexpected Joy you provided. On top of that you will be excited because you get to do it again tomorrow!

It's a lot more fun to be excellent than mediocre.

Ladies and Gentlemen,
LET'S HAVE FUN OUT THERE!